Two-thirds of the world is covered with oceans.
Only 5 percent have been explored.

For thousands of years, seafaring people have reported seeing fantastic creatures, biting beasts, and even glowing monsters able to sink the biggest ship.

But most of what inhabits the deepest parts of the ocean remains a mystery.

What's down there? There is only one way to find out . . .

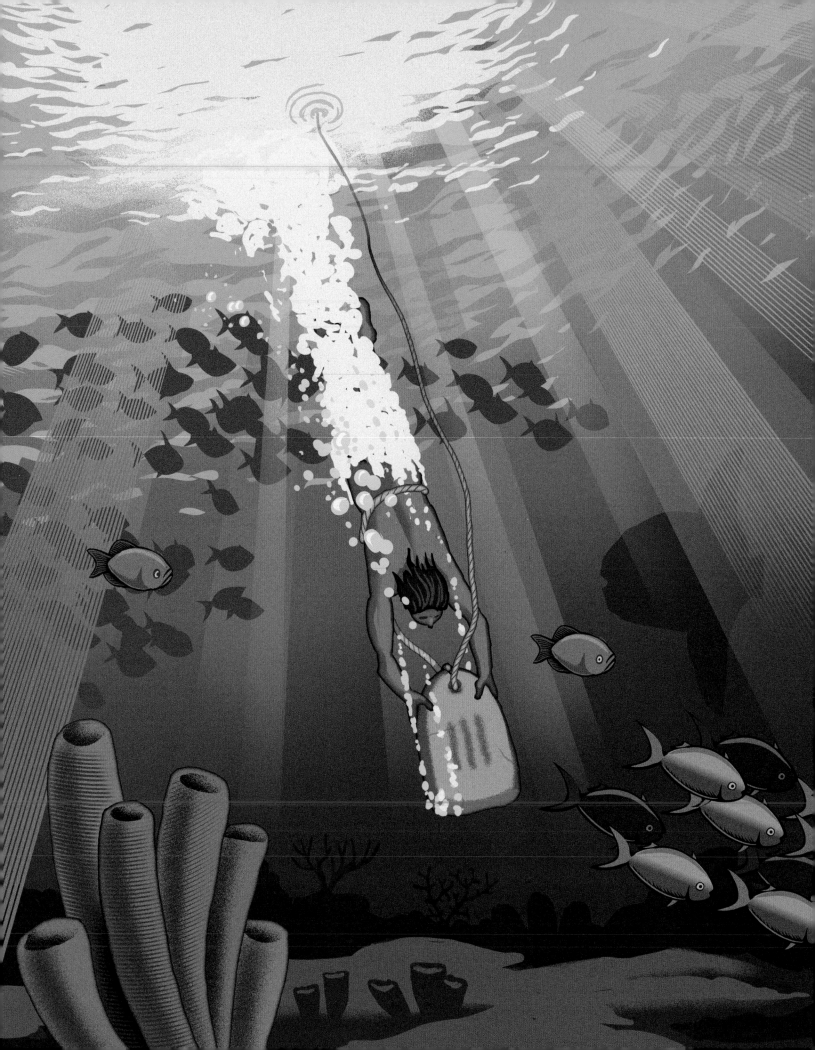

DIVE!

THE STORY OF
BREATHING UNDERWATER

CHRIS GALL

Roaring Brook Press

New York

Humans have always needed the sea. Around 2,400 years ago, the ancient Greeks used *sponges* for bathing and cleaning. They were not the sponges you might see in your kitchen, but living creatures that resided at the bottom of the ocean. They thrived at depths as deep as 200 feet, and the Greeks needed a way to dive down and get them.

Early sponge divers would hold their breath and jump from a boat while clutching a heavy stone called a *skandalopetra*. This helped them sink down to the bottom quickly. Both the diver and the stone were tied to a rope, and when the diver cut the sponges free and could no longer hold their breath, they would tug on the rope, and people in the boat pulled them up. Even the experienced diver could only hold their breath for around five minutes.

The ancient Greeks also found a way to breathe underwater. They would use hollow reeds as straws to hide underwater and avoid detection from enemies or stay under the surface longer in order to explore the ocean environment. However, if the reed was too long, the *pressure* of the water would not allow the diver to inhale *air*.

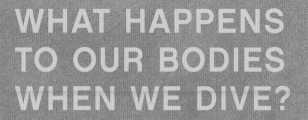

WHAT HAPPENS TO OUR BODIES WHEN WE DIVE?

Water is actually very heavy. As you dive deeper down, you are surrounded by more water as its weight squeezes your body. Because the majority of our bodies is liquid (60 percent water), a diver will not actually feel the water pressure around them, because the liquid in our bodies maintains equal pressure with the water outside our bodies. However, our bodies also have air spaces inside, and the water pressure will affect those. Lungs and intestines will shrink, but the spaces inside your ears and head will not, and this will be painful as you go deeper.

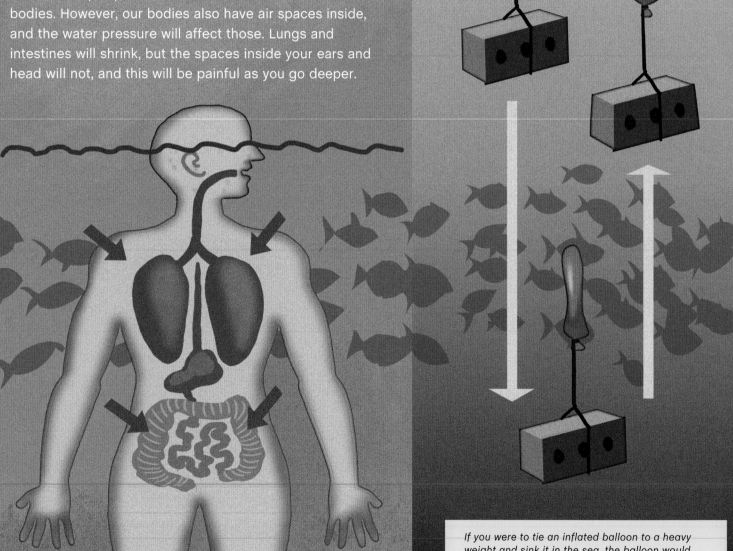

If you were to tie an inflated balloon to a heavy weight and sink it in the sea, the balloon would begin to shrink the deeper you went. Eventually, it would be crushed by the increasing water pressure. However, when you brought the balloon back up, it would re-inflate just like it was before. Our lungs and intestines are like the balloon: They will shrink or expand depending on how much water pressure is surrounding them. Unfortunately, our ears are a little different.

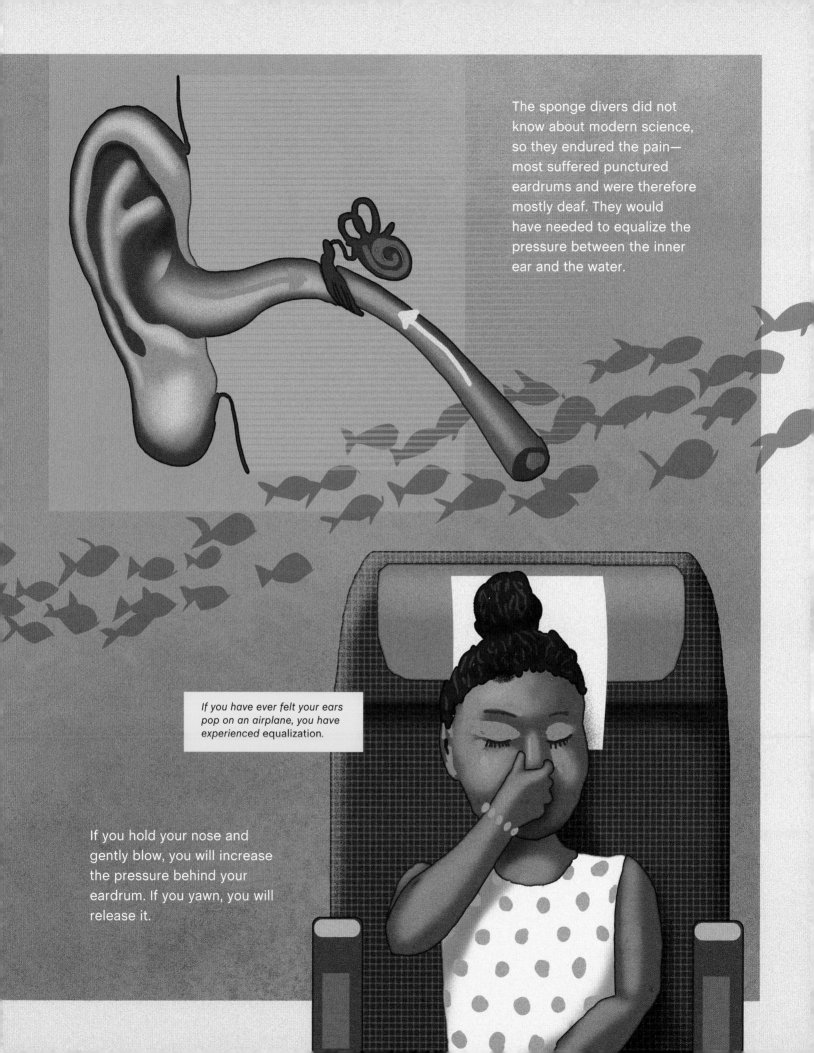

The sponge divers did not know about modern science, so they endured the pain—most suffered punctured eardrums and were therefore mostly deaf. They would have needed to equalize the pressure between the inner ear and the water.

If you have ever felt your ears pop on an airplane, you have experienced equalization.

If you hold your nose and gently blow, you will increase the pressure behind your eardrum. If you yawn, you will release it.

As societies developed, people realized they needed to stay underwater longer so they could do more work, like recovering sunken treasure or setting logs for docks. They needed to find a way to bring more air down with them.

Take an empty glass and turn it upside down. Now push it into a sink filled with water. You might expect the glass to fill up with water, but it doesn't. The air from the environment stays trapped inside the glass. You have just created a *diving bell*, which Aristotle, an ancient philosopher, first described in 400 BC.

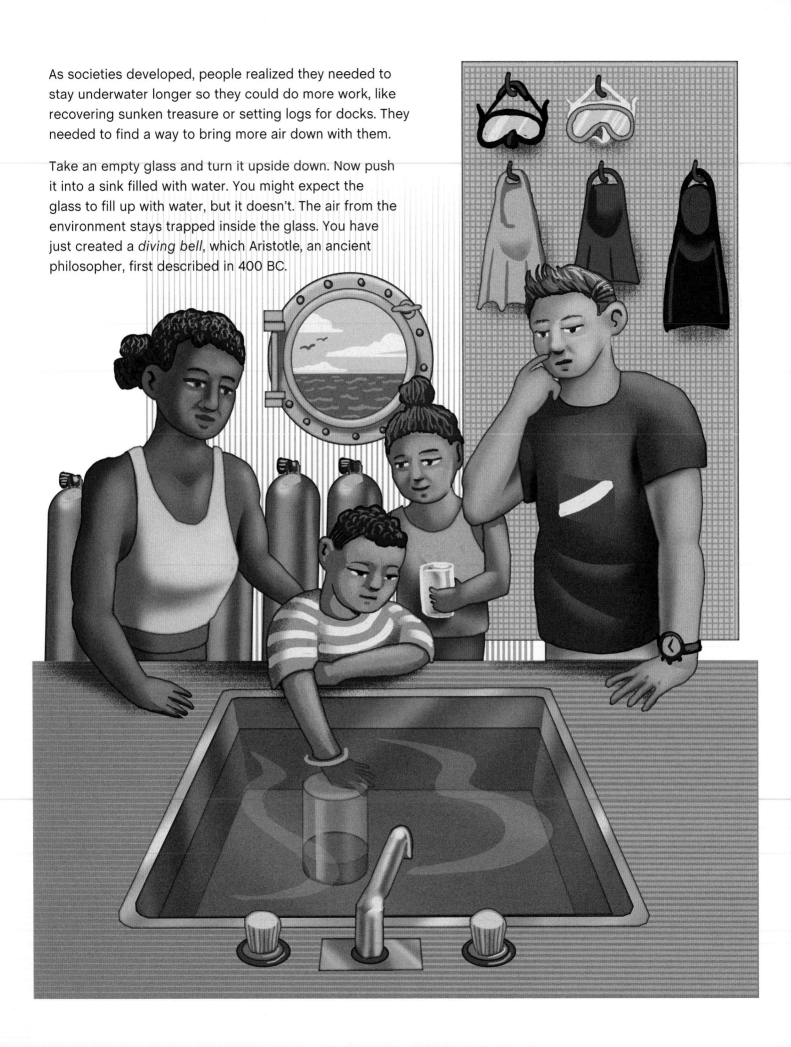

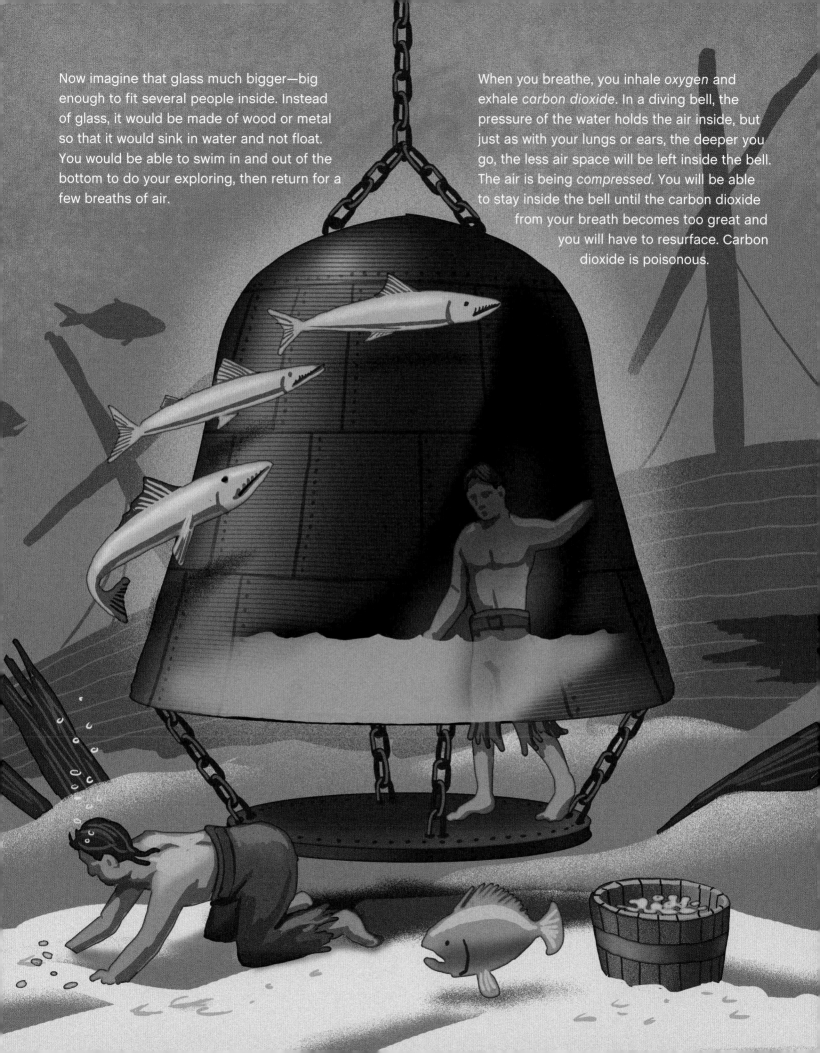

Now imagine that glass much bigger—big enough to fit several people inside. Instead of glass, it would be made of wood or metal so that it would sink in water and not float. You would be able to swim in and out of the bottom to do your exploring, then return for a few breaths of air.

When you breathe, you inhale *oxygen* and exhale *carbon dioxide*. In a diving bell, the pressure of the water holds the air inside, but just as with your lungs or ears, the deeper you go, the less air space will be left inside the bell. The air is being *compressed*. You will be able to stay inside the bell until the carbon dioxide from your breath becomes too great and you will have to resurface. Carbon dioxide is poisonous.

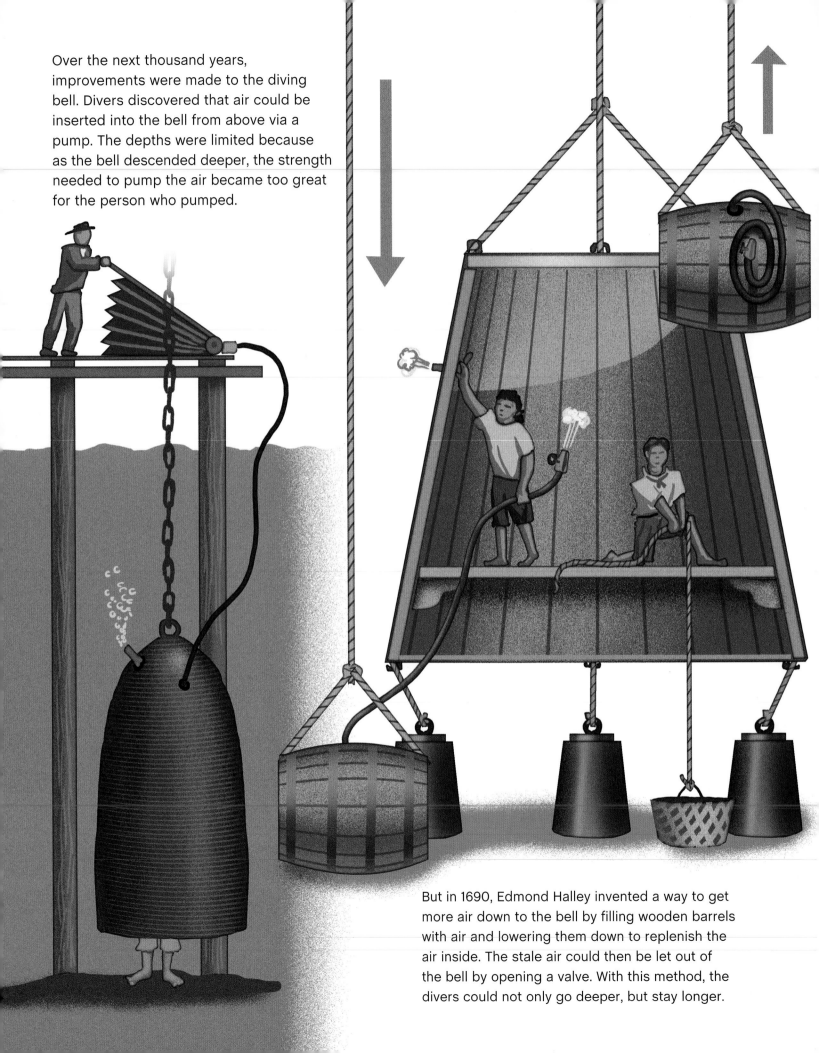

Over the next thousand years, improvements were made to the diving bell. Divers discovered that air could be inserted into the bell from above via a pump. The depths were limited because as the bell descended deeper, the strength needed to pump the air became too great for the person who pumped.

But in 1690, Edmond Halley invented a way to get more air down to the bell by filling wooden barrels with air and lowering them down to replenish the air inside. The stale air could then be let out of the bell by opening a valve. With this method, the divers could not only go deeper, but stay longer.

When you pump up a pool toy, you are using a simple air compressor.

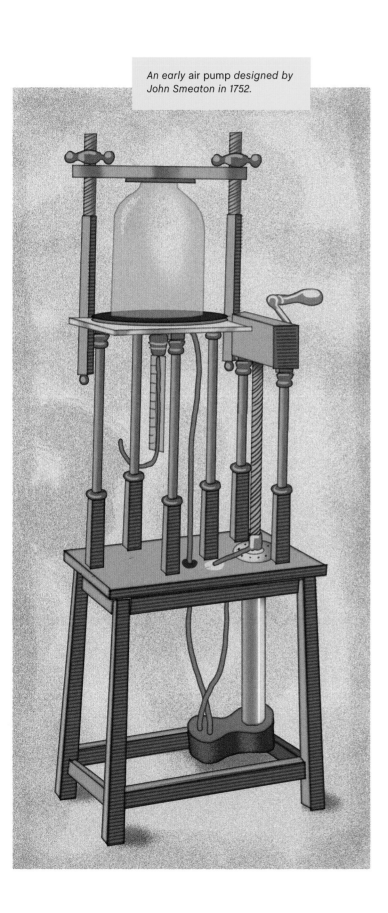

An early air pump designed by John Smeaton in 1752.

While these techniques were a good leap forward, working deeper meant increased air pressure. The increased air pressure caused more problems for divers, who often experienced burst eardrums and other painful symptoms from the pressure just like the early the sponge divers.

And there were to be more problems that went along with breathing compressed air.

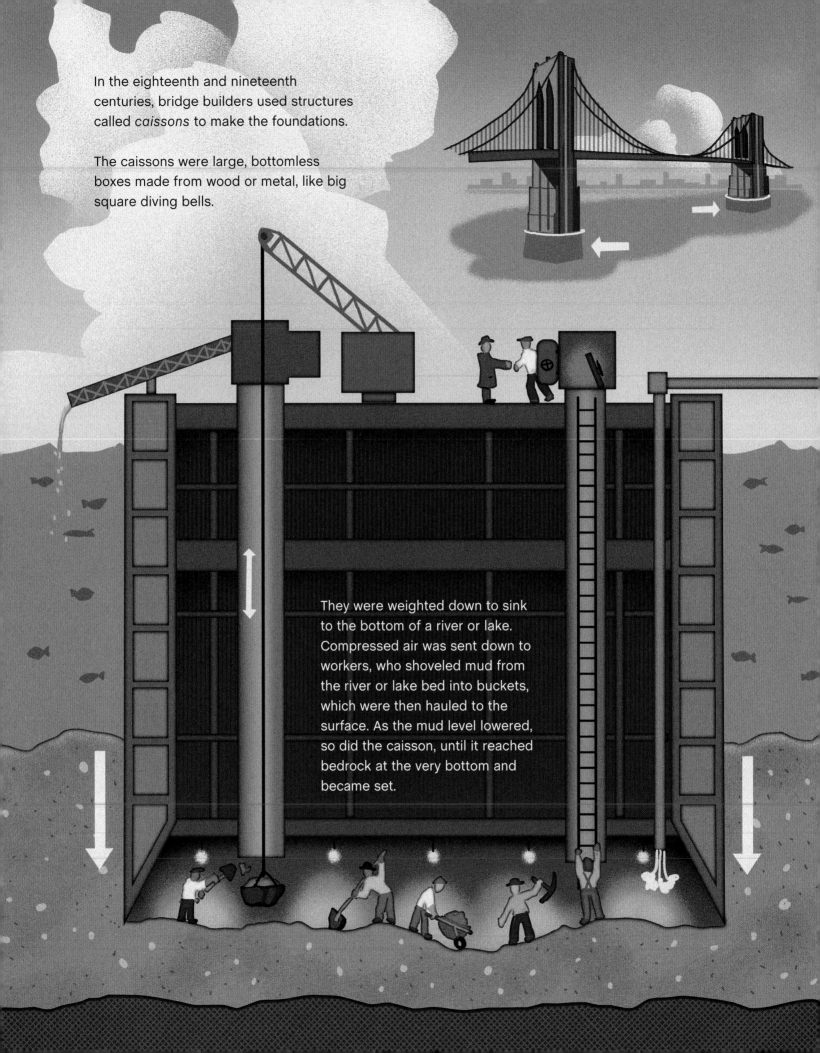

In the eighteenth and nineteenth centuries, bridge builders used structures called *caissons* to make the foundations.

The caissons were large, bottomless boxes made from wood or metal, like big square diving bells.

They were weighted down to sink to the bottom of a river or lake. Compressed air was sent down to workers, who shoveled mud from the river or lake bed into buckets, which were then hauled to the surface. As the mud level lowered, so did the caisson, until it reached bedrock at the very bottom and became set.

The caissons allowed for the construction of bigger, stronger bridges, but the workers often began getting sick when they returned to the surface. Severe joint pain would cause the workers to bend over in agony, leading doctors to call the condition *the bends*.

Nobody could figure out what was causing this disease, but they did observe that if the workers immediately returned to the caisson, the pains disappeared.

THE PROBLEM
WITH THE BENDS

In 1870, French doctor Paul Bert was the first to discover the cause of the bends, now called *decompression sickness*. When you breathe air, oxygen is used by your cells and *nitrogen* is dissolved into your blood and tissues. When you breathe compressed air, much more of the gas is dissolved into your body. If you suddenly go back to breathing normal air, at normal air pressure, the nitrogen doesn't have time to clear out of your body slowly—instead, it forms bubbles in your body. And this is what can lead to severe pain, especially in the joints. It can even cause paralysis and death.

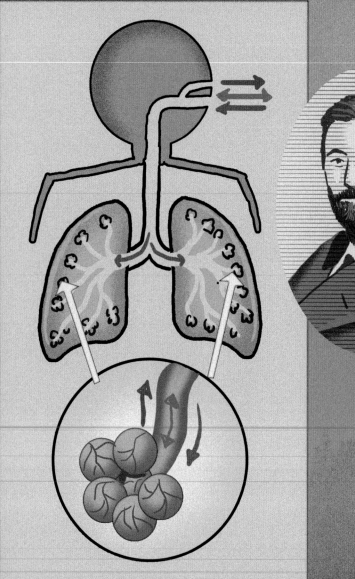

Dr. Bert realized that once a diver had breathed compressed air (typically pumped into a caisson from above) at a deep depth for even a modest amount of time, they would have to *slowly* decrease the pressure of the air (normally by going up) and allow time for the nitrogen to come out of the body through the breath. The longer the diver was down, the more time the diver would need on the trip up. This was called *decompression*, and the technique is still used today.

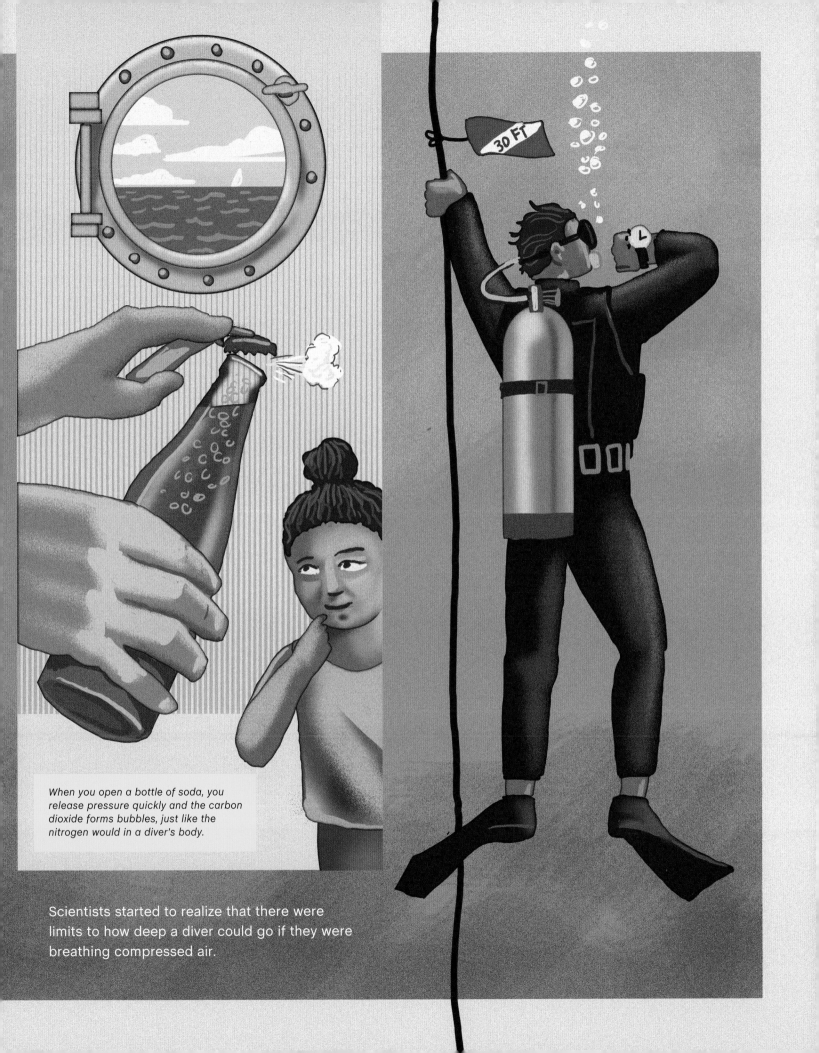

When you open a bottle of soda, you release pressure quickly and the carbon dioxide forms bubbles, just like the nitrogen would in a diver's body.

Scientists started to realize that there were limits to how deep a diver could go if they were breathing compressed air.

Divers were still looking for ways to be more mobile underwater and to be less reliant on a big diving bell. They wanted more freedom to explore.

In 1820, a man named John Deane watched as a farm near his home in England caught fire. The smoke in the barn was so thick that the fire brigade could not enter to save the horses that were trapped inside. Deane quickly borrowed a medieval helmet from a suit of armor on display nearby, and the firemen pumped air into it from a hose. The air kept the smoke out, and Deane was able to rescue the animals.

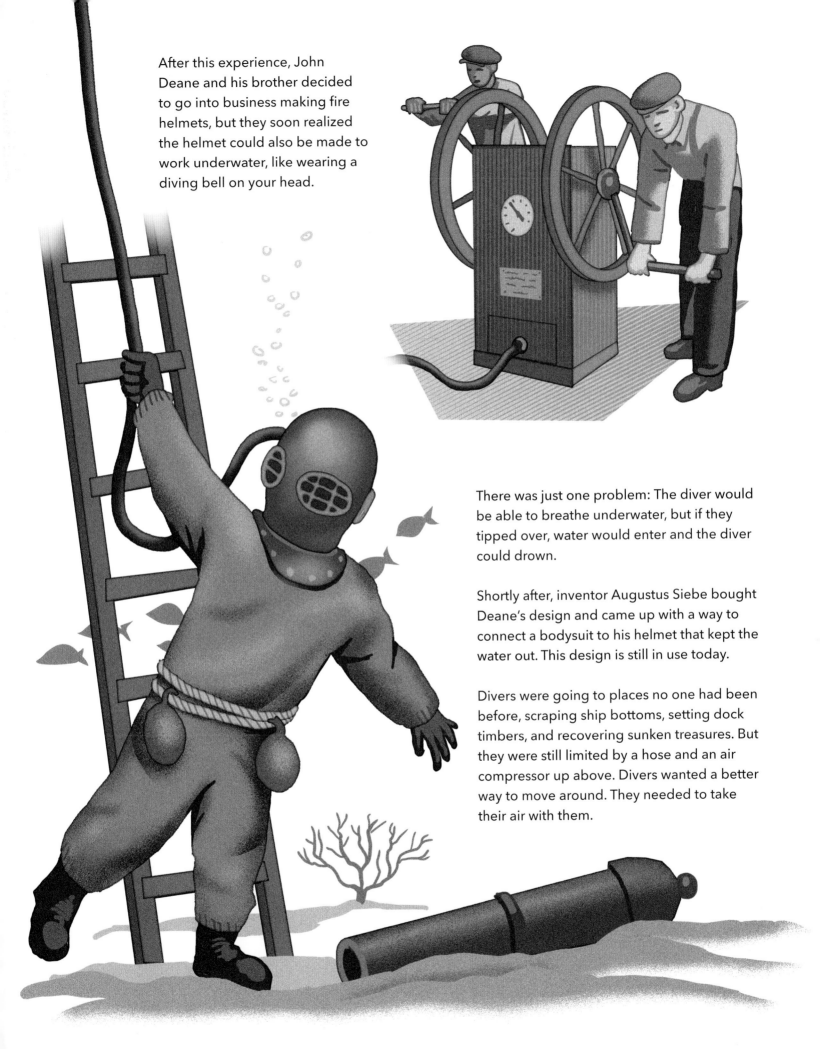

After this experience, John Deane and his brother decided to go into business making fire helmets, but they soon realized the helmet could also be made to work underwater, like wearing a diving bell on your head.

There was just one problem: The diver would be able to breathe underwater, but if they tipped over, water would enter and the diver could drown.

Shortly after, inventor Augustus Siebe bought Deane's design and came up with a way to connect a bodysuit to his helmet that kept the water out. This design is still in use today.

Divers were going to places no one had been before, scraping ship bottoms, setting dock timbers, and recovering sunken treasures. But they were still limited by a hose and an air compressor up above. Divers wanted a better way to move around. They needed to take their air with them.

In the late 1800s, the first practical system for breathing portable air was introduced.

It was called a *closed-circuit* system. This system carried a small oxygen tank and made no bubbles, which made it perfect for underwater observation and stealth. Just like on the surface, the diver breathed in the oxygen and exhaled carbon dioxide and unused oxygen. But instead of the expelled air going out into the water, a chemical within the device would absorb the poisonous carbon dioxide. Then a small amount of oxygen would be added from the tank, allowing the divers to rebreathe their own air. This machine was nicknamed a *rebreather*. Divers could now roam freely underwater, and a whole new world was waiting to be discovered.

Rebreathers today are often used for the study of marine life (where bubbles might scare the wildlife) and for secret naval missions. The technology is even used on spacecraft and submarines. But the early rebreathers could be complicated and dangerous, and there were other inventors who were eager to create a simpler device.

Early rebreather design by Fleuss for Siebe Gorman & Co.

Not all diving inventions were designed for the individual diver. In 1934, inventors and amateur divers Otis Barton and William Beebe set a record by diving 3,028 feet in a special craft they called a *bathysphere*. The divers sat inside a special container that was strong enough to resist crushing pressures, and thus could provide air to breathe at normal pressures using a rebreather.

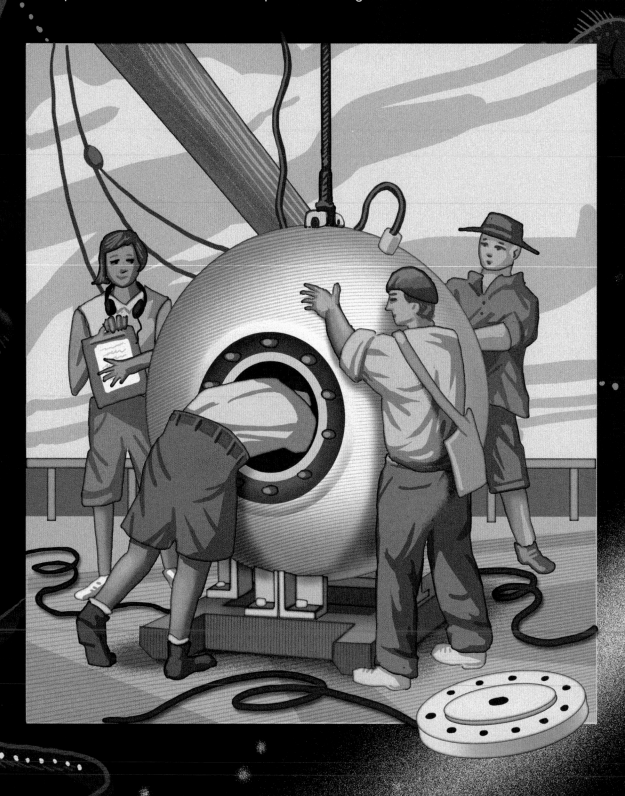

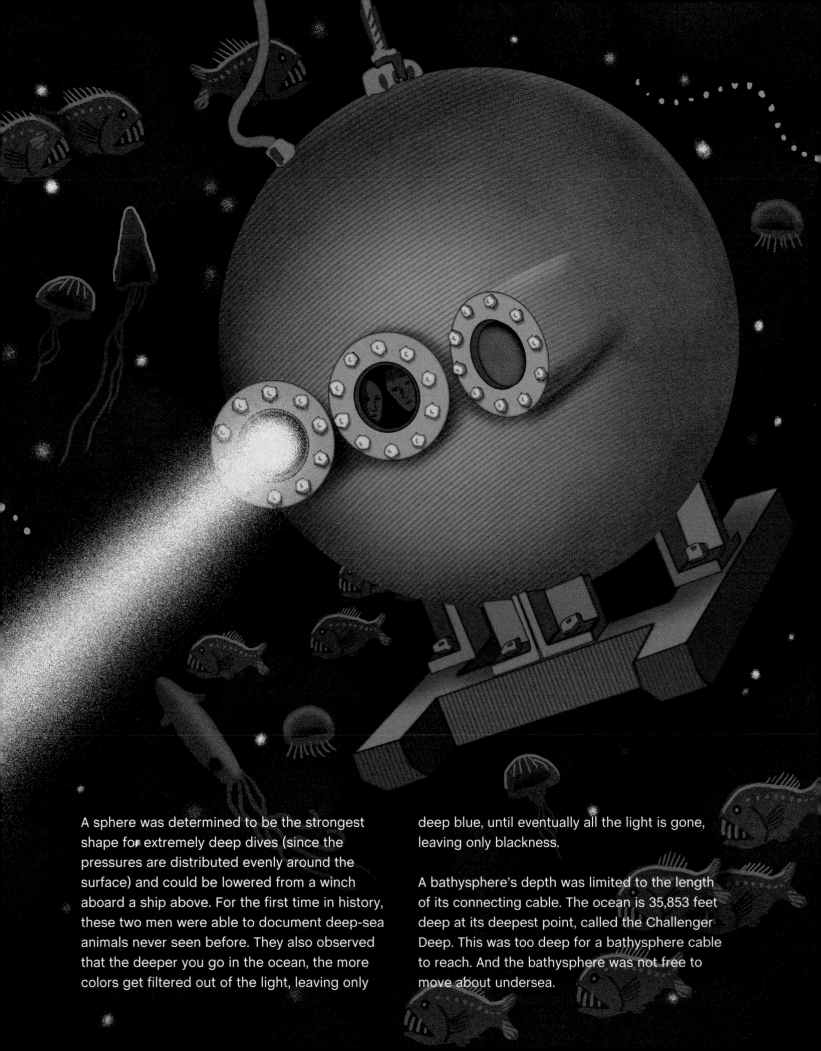

A sphere was determined to be the strongest shape for extremely deep dives (since the pressures are distributed evenly around the surface) and could be lowered from a winch aboard a ship above. For the first time in history, these two men were able to document deep-sea animals never seen before. They also observed that the deeper you go in the ocean, the more colors get filtered out of the light, leaving only

deep blue, until eventually all the light is gone, leaving only blackness.

A bathysphere's depth was limited to the length of its connecting cable. The ocean is 35,853 feet deep at its deepest point, called the Challenger Deep. This was too deep for a bathysphere cable to reach. And the bathysphere was not free to move about undersea.

The Aqua-Lung

In 1943, famous oceanographer Jacques Cousteau and his friend Émile Gagnan imagined a container to take regular air with them so they could swim freely underwater. The more air they carried, the longer they could stay underwater, so the air would have to be compressed, and there would need to be a way for this high-pressure air to get to their lungs without exploding them.

Cousteau and Gagnon had the idea to improve upon a breathing device commonly used for mine rescues. They created a special valve they called a *demand regulator*. This amazing invention was able to feed more air into a diver's lungs the deeper they went. In this way, the diver's lung pressure would always equal the outside water pressure, no matter how deep they were. Divers could breathe easily as the water pressure increased.

They called their new device the *Aqua-Lung*. A tank or two would be strapped to the diver's back, and now, with the invention of the face mask and swim fins, a diver could travel freely underwater.

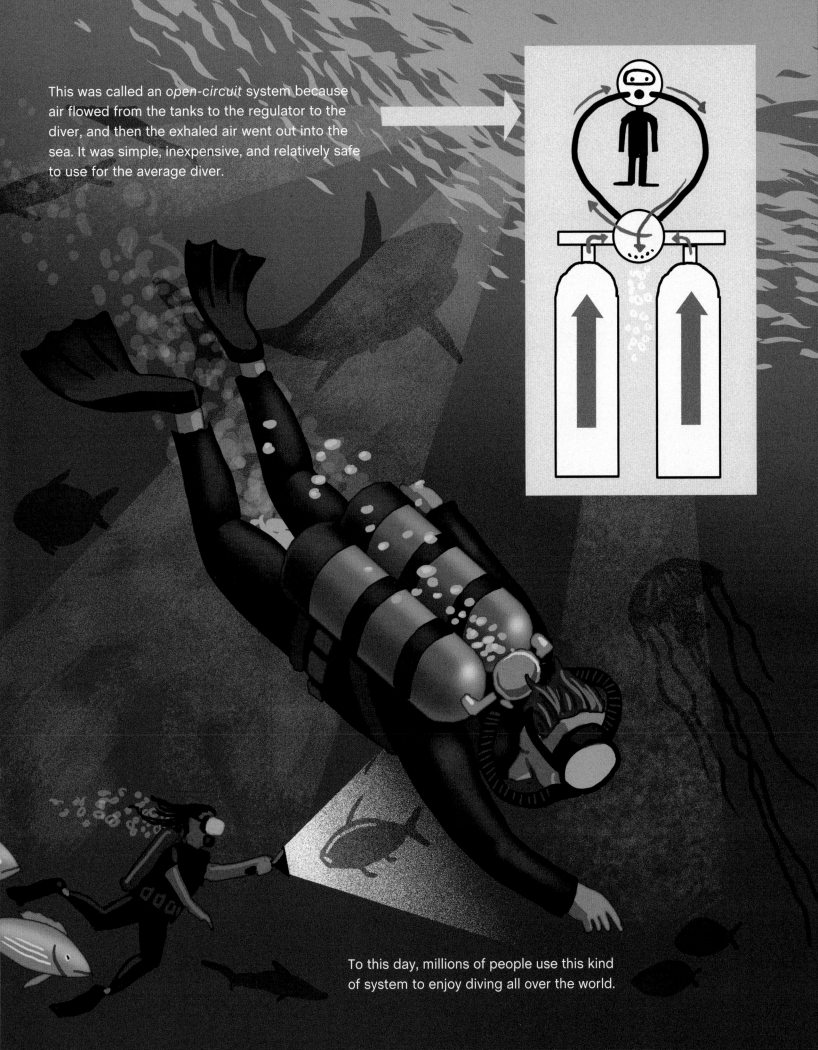

This was called an *open-circuit* system because air flowed from the tanks to the regulator to the diver, and then the exhaled air went out into the sea. It was simple, inexpensive, and relatively safe to use for the average diver.

To this day, millions of people use this kind of system to enjoy diving all over the world.

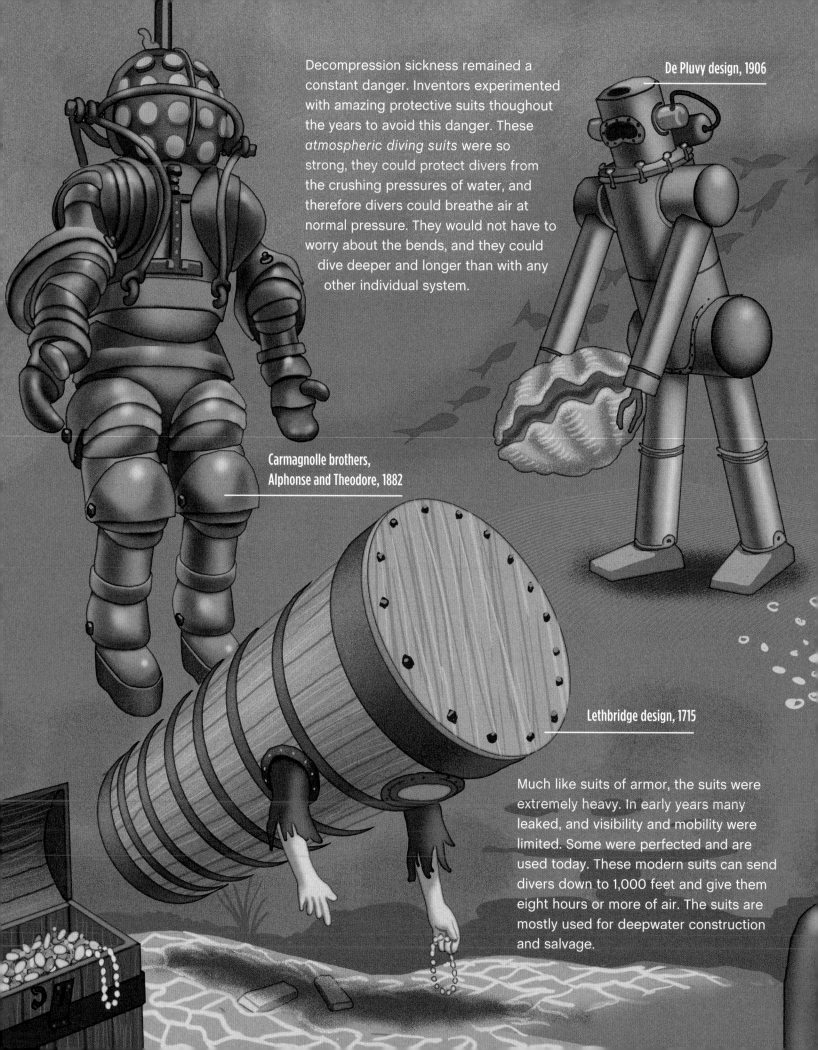

Decompression sickness remained a constant danger. Inventors experimented with amazing protective suits thoughout the years to avoid this danger. These *atmospheric diving suits* were so strong, they could protect divers from the crushing pressures of water, and therefore divers could breathe air at normal pressure. They would not have to worry about the bends, and they could dive deeper and longer than with any other individual system.

De Pluvy design, 1906

Carmagnolle brothers, Alphonse and Theodore, 1882

Lethbridge design, 1715

Much like suits of armor, the suits were extremely heavy. In early years many leaked, and visibility and mobility were limited. Some were perfected and are used today. These modern suits can send divers down to 1,000 feet and give them eight hours or more of air. The suits are mostly used for deepwater construction and salvage.

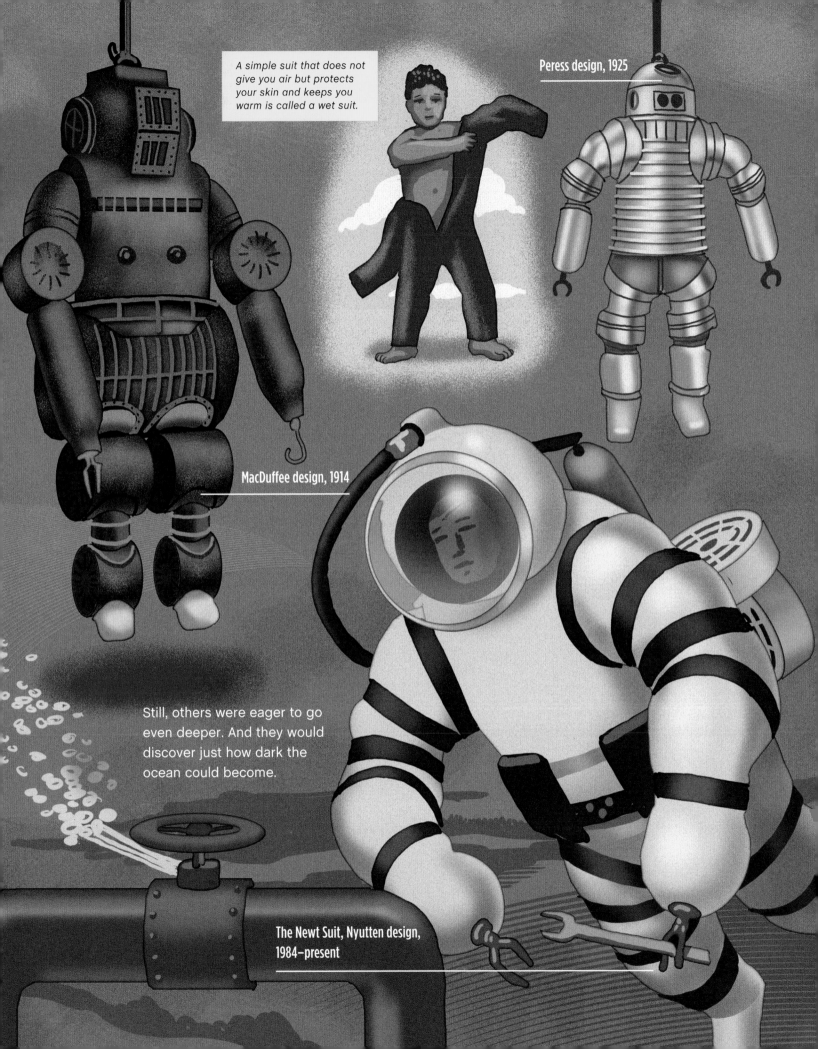

A simple suit that does not give you air but protects your skin and keeps you warm is called a wet suit.

Peress design, 1925

MacDuffee design, 1914

Still, others were eager to go even deeper. And they would discover just how dark the ocean could become.

The Newt Suit, Nyutten design, 1984–present

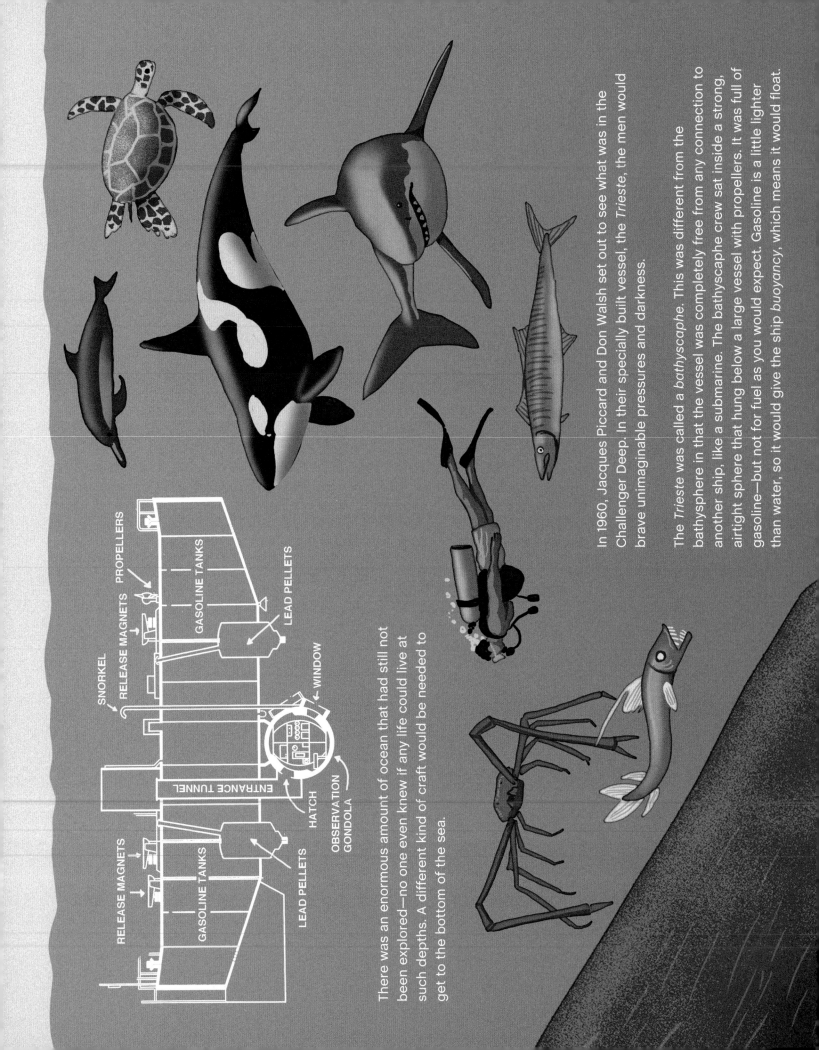

In 1960, Jacques Piccard and Don Walsh set out to see what was in the Challenger Deep. In their specially built vessel, the *Trieste*, the men would brave unimaginable pressures and darkness.

The *Trieste* was called a *bathyscaphe*. This was different from the bathysphere in that the vessel was completely free from any connection to another ship, like a submarine. The bathyscaphe crew sat inside a strong, airtight sphere that hung below a large vessel with propellers. It was full of gasoline—but not for fuel as you would expect. Gasoline is a little lighter than water, so it would give the ship *buoyancy*, which means it would float.

There was an enormous amount of ocean that had still not been explored—no one even knew if any life could live at such depths. A different kind of craft would be needed to get to the bottom of the sea.

PROPELLERS

RELEASE MAGNETS

GASOLINE TANKS

LEAD PELLETS

SNORKEL

WINDOW

ENTRANCE TUNNEL

HATCH

OBSERVATION GONDOLA

LEAD PELLETS

GASOLINE TANKS

RELEASE MAGNETS

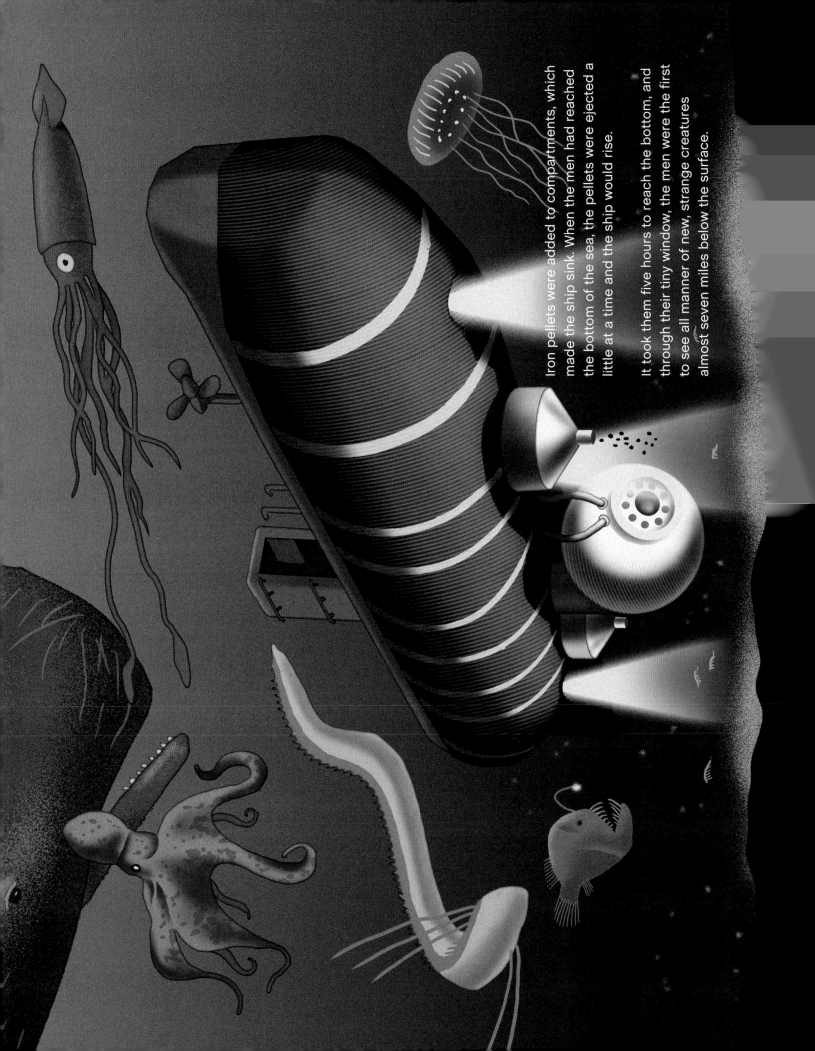

Iron pellets were added to compartments, which made the ship sink. When the men had reached the bottom of the sea, the pellets were ejected a little at a time and the ship would rise.

It took them five hours to reach the bottom, and through their tiny window, the men were the first to see all manner of new, strange creatures almost seven miles below the surface.

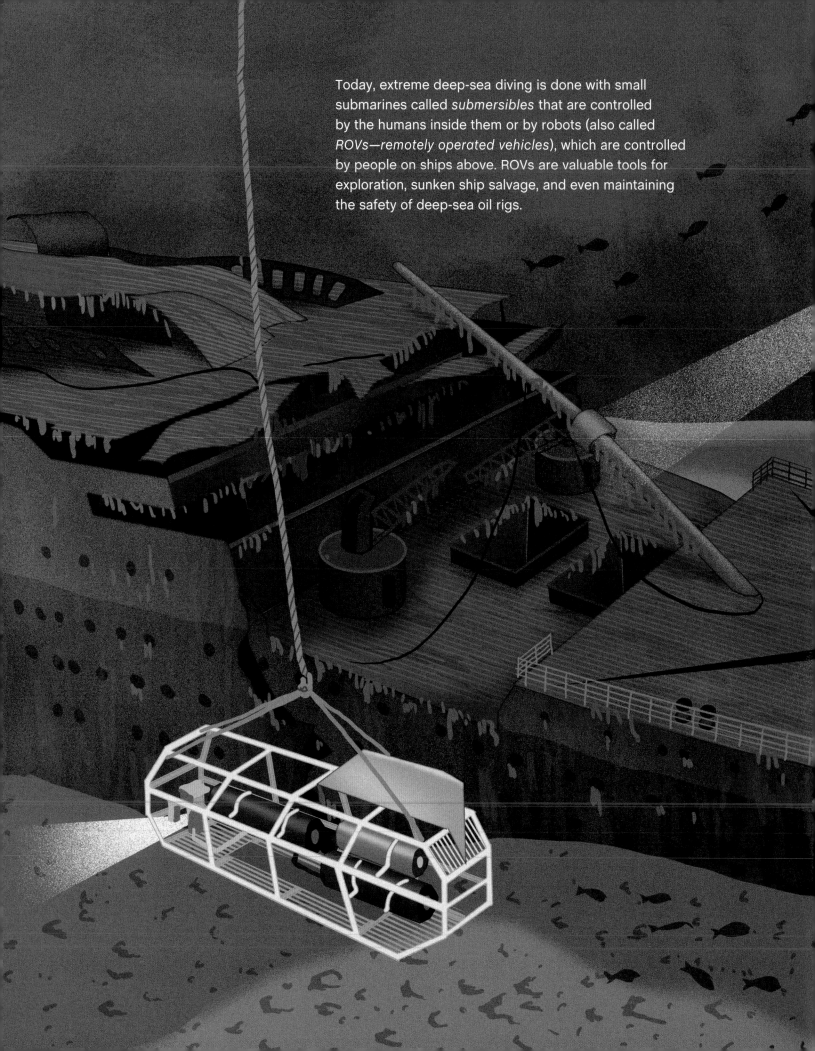

Today, extreme deep-sea diving is done with small submarines called *submersibles* that are controlled by the humans inside them or by robots (also called *ROVs—remotely operated vehicles*), which are controlled by people on ships above. ROVs are valuable tools for exploration, sunken ship salvage, and even maintaining the safety of deep-sea oil rigs.

The wreck of the *Titanic* was discovered with an ROV named *Argo*, and then was later explored with a submersible named *Alvin*. The ship was broken into pieces 12,500 feet below the surface!

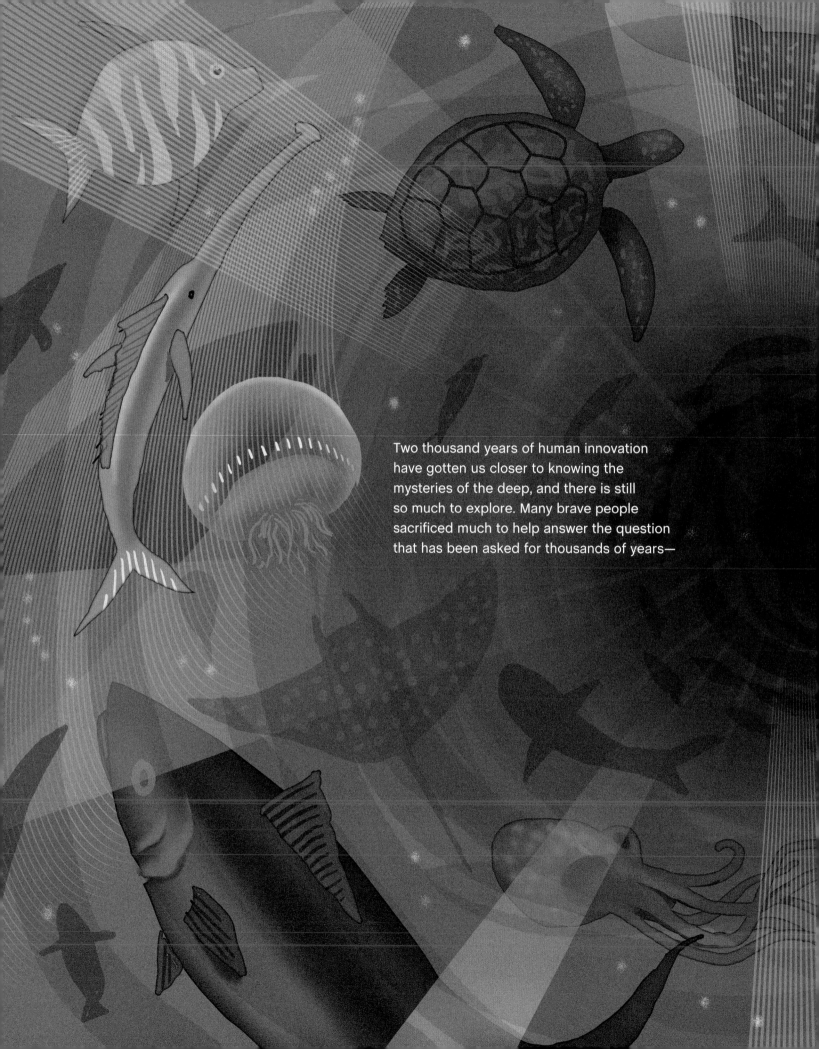

Two thousand years of human innovation have gotten us closer to knowing the mysteries of the deep, and there is still so much to explore. Many brave people sacrificed much to help answer the question that has been asked for thousands of years—

WHAT'S DOWN THERE?

OUR PRECIOUS OCEANS

The sea—vast, dark, and mysterious—has always been a part of us. The very first life-forms on Earth may have originated near underwater sea vents billions of years ago, giving rise to every living thing on the planet. We are, literally, born of the sea. We love our beaches and the sand between our toes. Tide pools, full of life, provide endless hours of wonder and exploration for people of all ages. And who could ever forget the warm breeze and a misty red sunset slowly dissolving into the horizon?

The ocean is a vital part of our planet's climate system. It helps keep the climate stable, and it absorbs much of the carbon dioxide that we produce. But as the planet warms up due to climate change, so do the oceans. Warmer water can cause problems for the creatures of the sea, humans, and the whole planet. Mass fish migrations change fishing grounds and disrupt food cycles, putting stress on many species. Coral reefs can't adjust to the temperatures and die off. Warmer water also causes toxic algal and bacterial blooms to increase, threatening fish, marine mammals, and even humans.

Overfishing is still a problem, with some species drastically reducing in numbers. Fish and seafood provide 17 percent of all animal protein consumed in the world, so further decreases in fish populations will only increase world hunger. Melting glaciers and ice caps will eventually raise ocean levels and threaten coastlines.

But there is still time to protect our oceans. Decreasing our dependence on fossil fuels and keeping plastics out of the water are just a start. Our seas are more than just vast bodies of water; they are key to our very survival.

WANT TO BECOME A DIVER?

Becoming a basic scuba diver is as challenging as it is exciting. You will have to be at least twelve years old, a good swimmer, and strong enough to carry the equipment you'll need. First, you will take classes at a certified dive school, where you will learn more about the many principles you discovered in this book! After you pass the written part of the test, it will be time to move to a controlled water environment, like a swimming pool. Here you will learn many basic safety skills, like taking your mask off and putting it back on and sharing your air with a dive buddy. Once you are comfortable breathing underwater, you will move to a natural body of water, like the ocean or a lake. Over two days you will complete four dives, each 60 feet deep, demonstrating to your instructor all you have learned. You will then be a certified diver!

RESOURCES

padi.com • naui.org

CAREERS IN DIVING

There are many exciting ways to make a career as a diver. Some of these include becoming an underwater photographer, a commercial diver (fixing and building underwater equipment), a dive instructor, or a marine archaeologist (they find sunken treasure!). People can even earn a living diving for golf balls on golf courses. After achieving your basic dive certificate, there are many more advanced courses you will be able to take, such as wreck diving, night diving, and learning to breathe other special gases besides normal air.

FUN FACTS

Coconuts are more dangerous than sharks. Falling coconuts kill an average of 150 people a year. Sharks kill an average of ten people a year.

On land, our ears can tell the direction of a sound because the sound is detected by one ear before the other. But sound moves five times faster underwater than in air. The speed of the passing sound makes it impossible for our ears to detect the difference in time, and therefore sounds underwater seem to come from any direction.

"Scuba" stands for "self-contained underwater breathing apparatus."

Around 94 percent of Earth's wildlife is found in the ocean.

The record for the world's deepest open-circuit scuba dive was set by Ahmed Gabr in 2014. It took him fifteen minutes to get down to 1,090 feet. He spent the next thirteen hours slowly ascending to avoid the bends.

The pressure exerted by the air around you is about 14 pounds per square inch. In the Challenger Deep (the deepest part of the ocean), the pressure on your body is 16,000 pounds per square inch!

The record for the world's deepest dive on one breath of air was set by Herbert Nitsch, who used a weighted sled to descend and a balloon to ascend. He reached 830 feet in depth.

Almost all (90 percent) of the world's volcanic activity takes place in the ocean.

Spitting into your mask and smearing the glass will help prevent the glass from fogging up.

If the amount of plastic that makes its way into the ocean keeps increasing, the plastic will weigh more than all the fish in the sea by 2050.

GLOSSARY

Air—what we breathe every day, composed primarily of oxygen and nitrogen

Air pump—a device used to compress air

Aqua-Lung—an economical device that allows a diver to carry their air with them as they swim

Bathyscaphe—a bathysphere that is attached to a self-propelled diving craft

Bathysphere—a self-contained diving craft lowered by cable into the sea

The bends—also known as decompression sickness; occurs when nitrogen gas, dissolved in the blood and tissues, is released into the body too quickly and forms bubbles, causing pain or death

Carbon dioxide—the gas that is emitted from your breath when you exhale

Caisson—a large, heavy box sunk into water to provide working space for bridge builders

Compression—occurs when pressure is exerted on a space of lower pressure, causing the space to shrink

Decompression—when someone who has been breathing compressed air slowly decreases the pressure to avoid the bends

Diving bell—a vessel that holds air for a diver to breathe

Equalization—combining the forces of two different pressures to create equal pressure

Nitrogen—a gas in the air that the body does not need for respiration

Oxygen—a gas in the air that humans need to live

Pressure—the force exerted, either by air or water, on the human body

Rebreather—the first device to allow a diver to move freely without being attached to an air hose

ROV (remotely operated vehicle)—an uncrewed undersea vehicle controlled by people on the surface

Skandalopetra—a heavy carved stone held by ancient divers to make them sink faster

Sponge—a type of simple undersea animal with many holes that trap food

SOURCES

"A Brief History of Diving: Free Divers, Bells and Helmets." *Dive Training*. Accessed May 12, 2023. dtmag.com/thelibrary/a-brief-history-of-diving-free-divers-bells-and-helmets/.

Aqualung. us.aqualung.com.

Emly, Bryce. "How the Diving Bell Opened the Ocean's Depths." *The Atlantic*, March 2017.

History of Diving Museum. divingmuseum.org.

PADI (Professional Association of Diving Instructors). padi.com.

Scuba.com.

Streever, Bill. *In Oceans Deep: Courage, Innovation, and Adventure Beneath the Waves*. New York: Little, Brown and Company, 2019.

AUTHOR'S NOTE

I was a diver.

Many years ago, off the coast of the Yucatán peninsula, I strapped on 30 pounds of gear, including enough air for at least forty minutes of breathing, and jumped into the sea. My dive instructor, Manuel, was taking me down 60 feet for my first open-water lesson.

I was nervous.

I had already attended classroom instruction, taken tests, and practiced in a swimming pool. But this was different. The sea swells were larger than I thought they would be, so I was eager to get underwater where the water was calm. I let air out of my buoyancy vest so I would slowly sink down, down, until my knees rested on the ocean floor.

I was focused on performing the skills I had practiced for my instructor. Take my mask off, put it back on. Take my tank off, put it back on. Control my breathing so that I would neither sink nor float. I needed to show I could hover in a way that kept me from harming the coral beneath me.

When it was time to take what Manuel called "a tour of the sea," I could finally relax a little, and we started to swim. Now I could take in the wonders of undersea life. Fish of every kind surrounded me. Jellyfish floated by as the sea fans gently swayed in the current. And then—right there! A school of a dozen barracuda glided by, their razor teeth gnashing and their big eyes rolling toward us. Luckily they were only mildly interested in our presence, and they continued on their way.

Then there were the sounds—clicks and grunts from shrimp, crackling noises from coral. And every now and then the distant squeaking of a porpoise or the low groan of a whale. I was on a foreign planet. I felt like a spaceman, flying slowly over an exotic landscape, seeing all manner of life-forms that I had never seen before. But I wasn't a spaceman. I was an explorer of the sea.

Published by Roaring Brook Press

Roaring Brook Press is a division of Holtzbrinck Publishing Holdings Limited Partnership

120 Broadway, New York, NY 10271 • mackids.com

Our books may be purchased in bulk for promotional, educational, or business use. Please contact your local bookseller or the Macmillan Corporate and Premium Sales Department at (800) 221-7945 ext. 5442 or by email at MacmillanSpecialMarkets@macmillan.com.

Library of Congress Cataloging-in-Publication Data is available.

First edition, 2024

The illustrations in this book were created on a Wacom drawing tablet, and the type was set in Avenir and Chalet. The book was edited by Emily Feinberg, with design by Mike Burroughs. The assistant editor was Emilia Sowersby. The production editor was Mia Moran, and the production was supervised by Elizabeth Peskin. Printed in China by RR Donnelley Asia Printing Solutions Ltd., Dongguan City, Guangdong Province

ISBN 978-1-250-82395-3

1 3 5 7 9 10 8 6 4 2